Shadowplay

Photographs by Marc Mainguy - Paris

Shadowplay

George Mendoza
with Prasanna Rao

Holt, Rinehart and Winston

New York Chicago San Francisco

A Holt Reinforced Edition

Copyright © 1974 by Ruth Diana Mendoza
All rights reserved, including the right
to reproduce this book or portions thereof
in any form.

Published simultaneously in Canada by
Holt, Rinehart and Winston of Canada, Limited.

Library of Congress Cataloging in Publication Data

Mendoza, George.
    Shadowplay.

    Summary: Photographs of shadow images of swans,
camels, Napoleon, witches, and other figures together with photographs showing how the images are
formed using hands and fingers.

    1. Shadow-pictures—Juvenile literature.
[1. Shadow pictures] I. Rao, Prasanna, joint author.
II. Mainguy, Marc, illus. III. Title.
GV1218.S5M46   791.5   72-9958
ISBN 0-03-007881-4 (lib. bdg.)

Printed in the United States of America

Designed by Earl Tidwell

First Edition

This work is dedicated to my friends, Samuel Beckett,
who understands the retreat of shadows,
and Alvin Ferleger,
the second greatest shadowcaster in the world . . . .

and with special thanks to Earl Tidwell.

Foreword

Besides drawing and painting on cave walls as a form of artistic expression, the caveman may well have cast shadows of himself on the walls by standing in front of a fire. To entertain his friends, he could have created shadows of animals on those walls by twisting his fingers and hands in imitation of them.

Although it is not known precisely where the art of shadows originated, an ancient Chinese legend tells of an emperor who, in a fit of rage, had his court jester beheaded. Regretting his rash act, he ordered the court magician to bring the jester back to life. Faced with this impossible request, the magician cut a likeness of the jester out of the skin of a fish and cast the shadow on a screen to impress and entertain the emperor.

The art of shadows as an amusement was a tradition in Chinese theater more than two thousand years ago. Puppets in shadow were used in royal ceremonies. Later, puppeteers traveled the countryside entertaining the public. Shadow shows were an art as well as an entertainment in China. As the shadow show began to spread westward across Asia, the form of shadowplay varied in technique. By the time it reached Europe, human (as opposed to puppet) shadows were being used to perform. During the reign of Queen Victoria in England, shadowplays were a popular form of home entertainment. In France, in the nineteenth century, this new art form was called *Ombres Chinoises*—"Chinese shadows."

The uses of shadow have not only had an incredible influence over many of our present forms of entertainment, but they have aided in our scientific understanding of the universe: Aristotle knew the earth was round because he saw its curved shadow on the moon during an eclipse; the shadows cast on the first sundials were our first clocks; early cartoons were shadow shows, and many cinematic films utilized moving silhouettes. Television sets are really only electric shadow boxes.

The art of shadowgraphy is the presentation of silhouetted images of characters on a screen with the help of the manipulation of hands and fingers—the shadows resemble persons, animals, or objects.

The art of shadowplay is the interaction of these characters to form a story or play. Many of the shadowgraphists of the past were also magicians, for, the shadow, like the tricks of magic, demands quickness of hand.

Hand shadows have one advantage over the shadow show or play—the creation of the images is entirely personal. Your shadow belongs to you, and what you do with it is a true expression of your individuality.

The combination of the ancient art of shadowplay and the technique of shadowgraphy creates a wonderful art form which has been cultivated by Prasanna Rao since his youth. Rao has devoted his life to popularizing this form of entertainment. He has performed on American television, as well as in cafes throughout Europe.

Prasanna Rao is a genius in the art of silhouette. An incredible sculptor of shadow, he molds his fingers and hands as though they were fluid. Rao has mastered his art, and, with patience, time, and effort, you will be able to imitate the hands of the master shadow sculptor and discover for yourself the world of shadowgraphy and shadowplay.

—*George Mendoza*

Note: In some cases a separate photograph was taken of the hands to more clearly show the correct arrangement of the fingers, which will account for a slight difference between the position of the hands and the shadow cast.

Rhinoceros

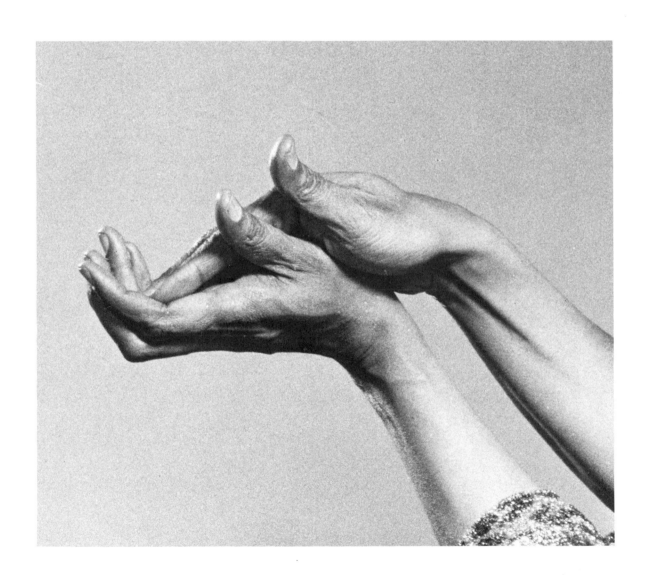

Rabbit

Horse

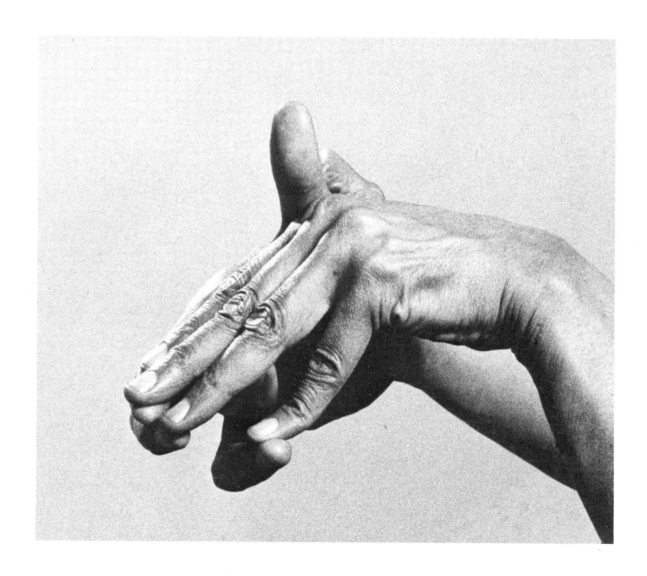

Elephant

Dog

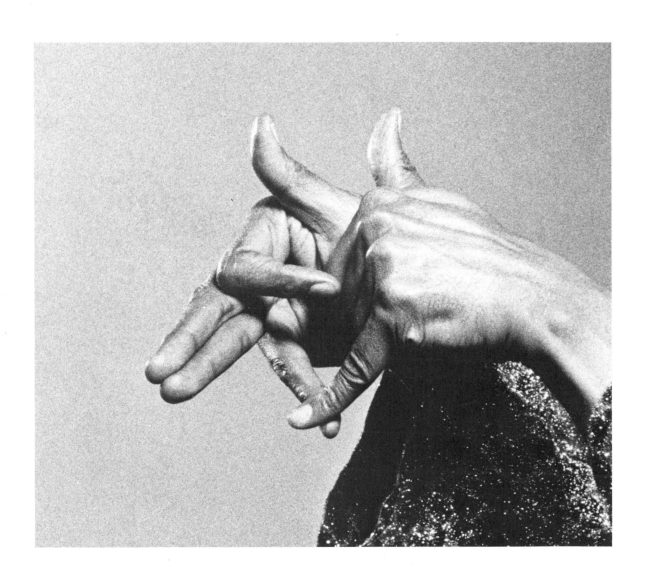

Eagle

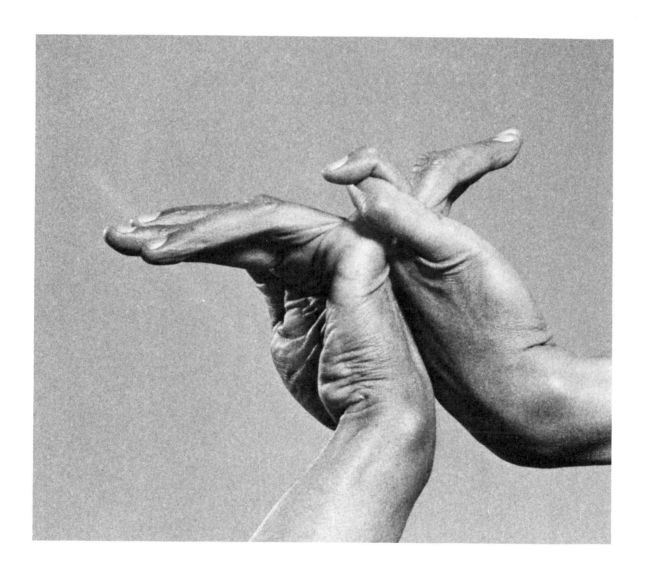

Puma

Goat

Camel

Donkey

Swan

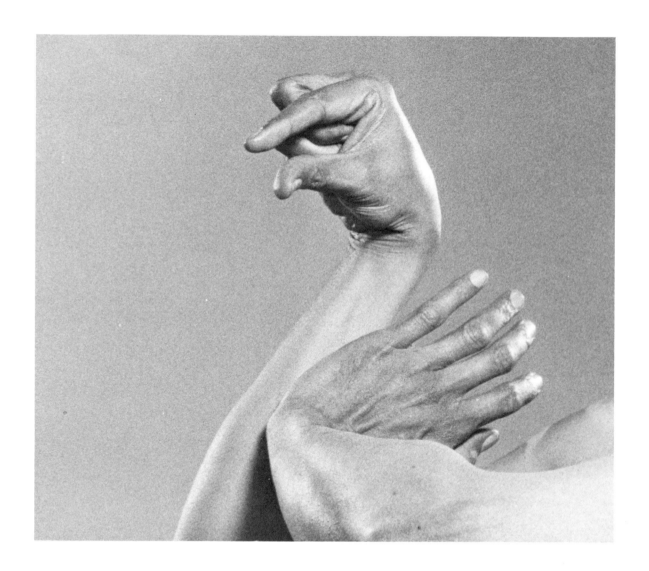

Giraffes

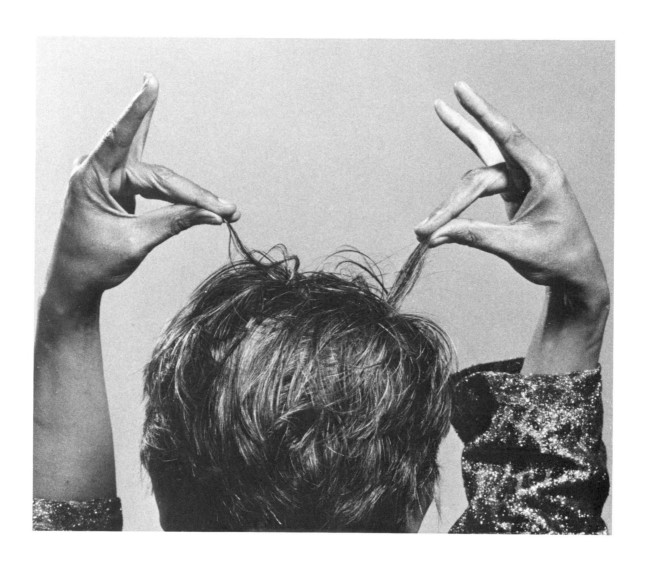

Cow

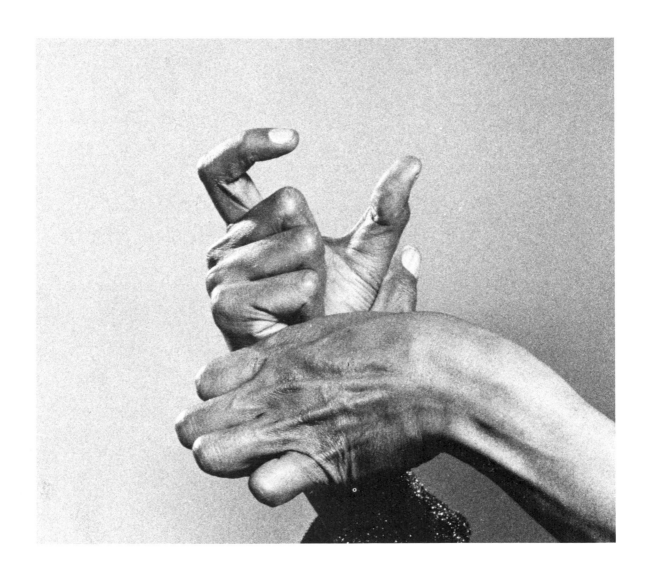

Moose

People in the park

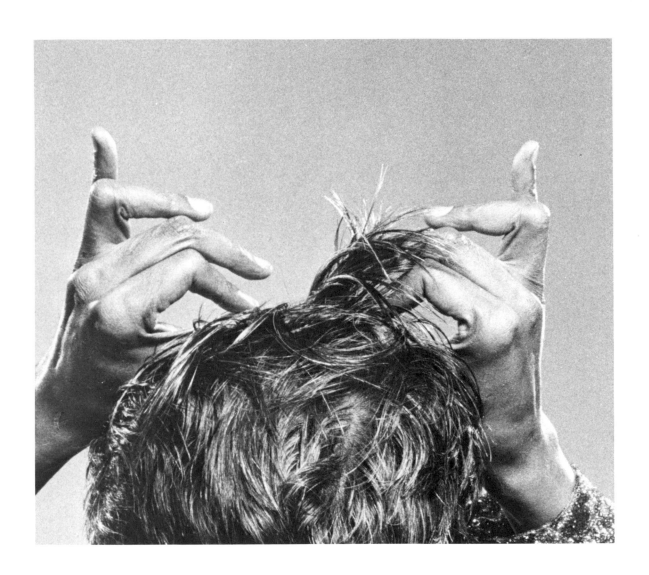

Man laughing

Man with moustache

Napoleon

Indian

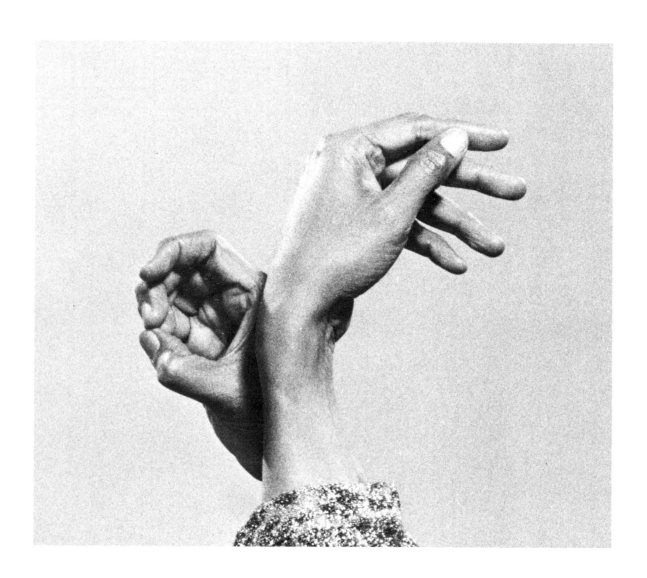

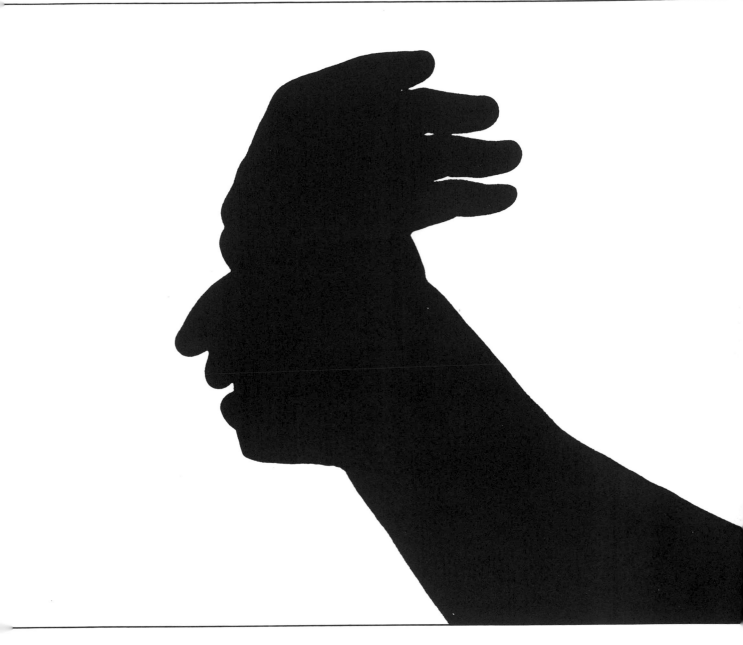

Man with cigar

Jockey

Witch

Taxi

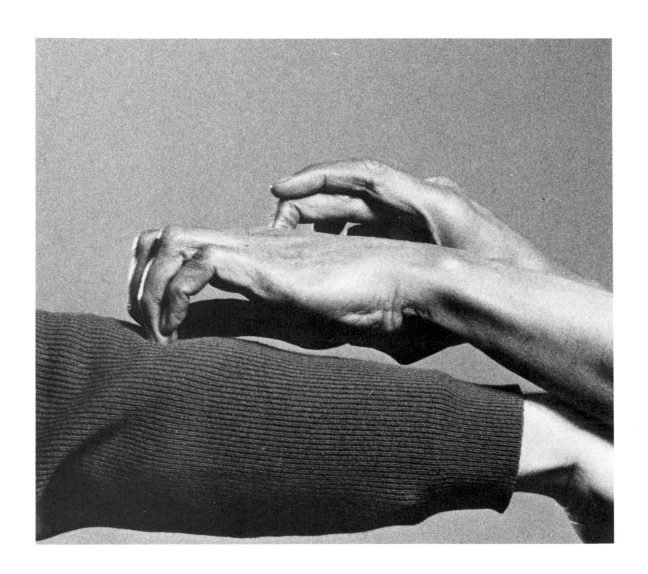

Taxi driver

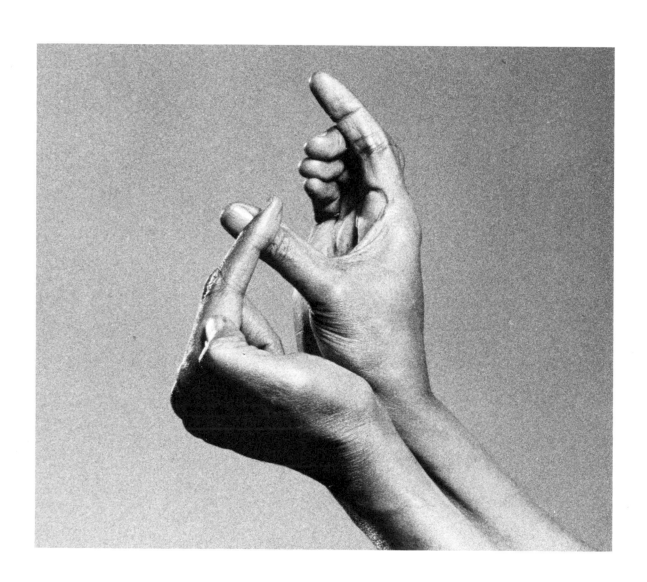

Flower

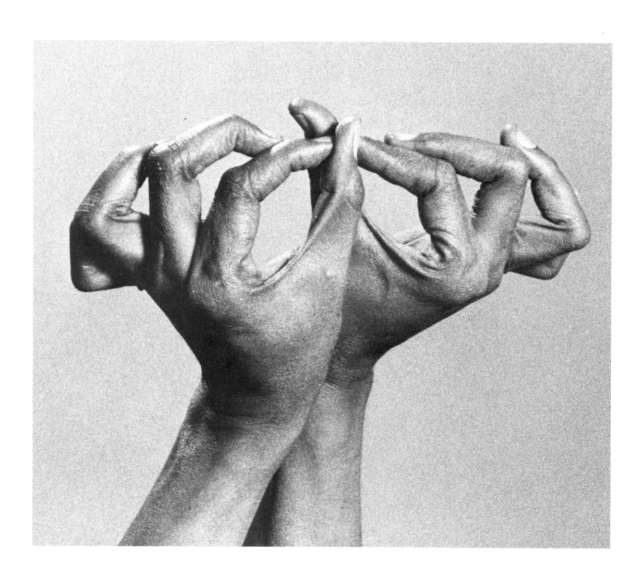

Teapot

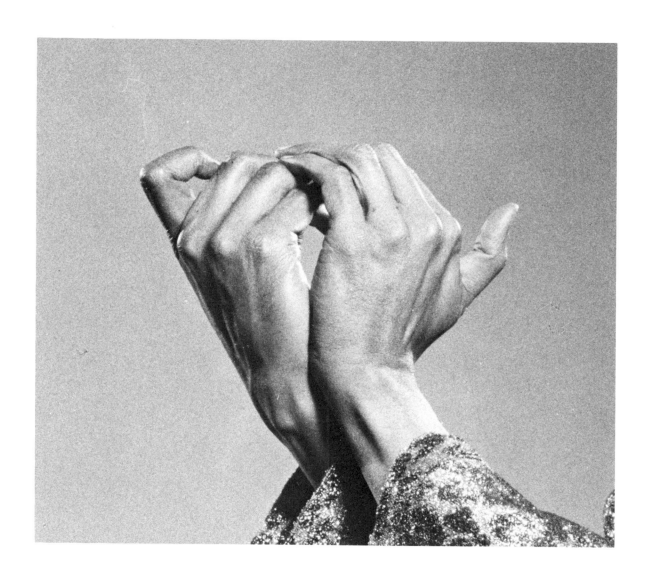

HAND EXERCISES

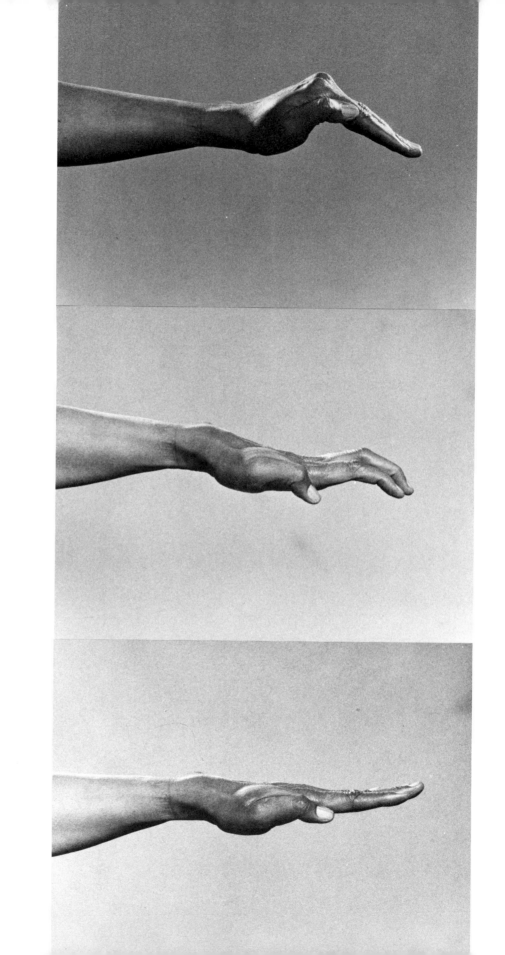

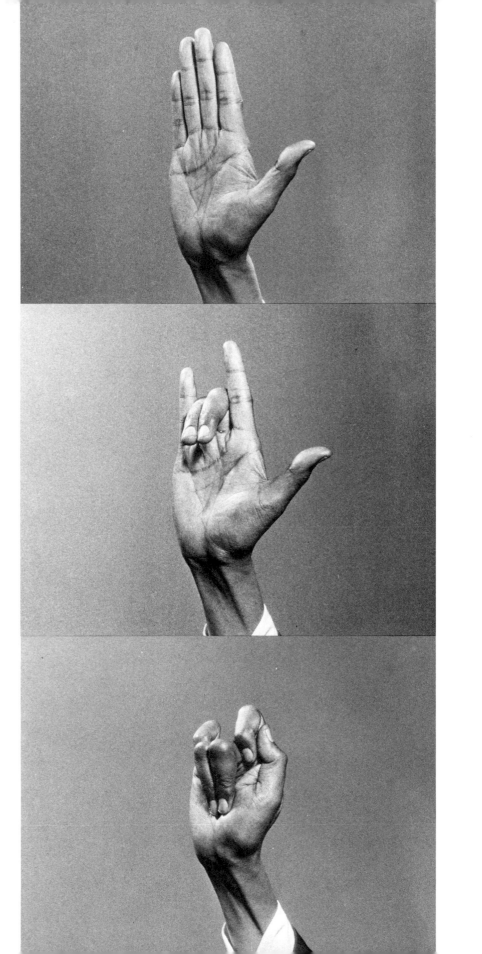

When Prasanna Rao was a little boy in India, he became very ill and had to remain in bed for long periods of time. To escape his loneliness, Rao created silhouette profiles of men, birds, and animals with his fingers and hands.

"As a sickly child, I was forced to stay in my bed. At night, when everyone was asleep, I practiced my shadows with a hurricane lamp."

Prasanna Rao has never stopped making shadows, and today, he is regarded throughout the world as the "Prince of Shadows."

George Mendoza met Rao in Paris, and together, they have created a definitive work on the art of shadowplay.